BATTLEFIELD HTML

BY Brian Manning

Copyright © 2013

Battlefield HTML Handbook

BATTLEFIELD HTML:
Markup in the Mean Streets..................................4

What Was All That About?......................................6

    The Tags You Just Used..7

Fundamentals of Battlefield HTML.....................10

    The New Tags..11

    Block Elements and Inline Elements..............................12

    The <img> Tag..13

    Develop Good Habits...15

Fundamentals of BATTLEFIELD CSS.................17

    The Style Tag.. 17

    CSS Properties..20

CSS Power and Flexibility..................................23

    The Mighty <div> Tag.. 26

    Let's Bring a Little Class to the Show..............................28

Battlefield Applications....................................... 31

    Site Template 1..32

    Site Template 2..44

CSS Background Images..................................53
The Sample Files..53
Extra Credit..56
index.html...56
ex3_style.css..58

Tags for Grown-up HTML................................60
Article and Section Tags................................61
Other Useful Tags..62

So, uh...What Now What?..............................67

Site Resources..68
Coding Tools..68

About the Author...70

Thank You!..72

BATTLEFIELD HTML:
Markup in the Mean Streets

I bet that title got your attention, huh? Alright, don't worry about what HTML is, or what you are about to do yet. If you are using Windows, open Notepad and create a new file. If you are using Mac, open TextEdit and from the "Format" pulldown menu, select "Make Plain Text" (You can also use the keyboard shortcut COMMAND + SHIFT + T). In Plain Text mode, there should be no tool bars or rulers on top. Now type the following (all of it, in this exact order):

```
<!DOCTYPE html>
<html>
<head>
   <title>BATTLEFIELD HTML: Markup in Mean
   Streets</title>
</head>

<body>
   You did it! You created your first web page!
</body>
</html>
```

Got all that? Are you sure? Good, save it as (file: save as...) "index.html". Preferably in a separate folder that you can find easily, and keep organized (not just on the desktop). Now just open up a web browser, like Internet Explorer, FireFox, Chrome, or Safari, like you would if you wanted to access other websites. From the file menu, select "Open File..." and choose your index.html file (you did put it somewhere easy to find, right?). Congratulations, you just made your first web page. Welcome to the war, kid.

Why are we calling the file "index.html"? What's all that stuff between the brackets? Does it have to be in that order? Please hold all questions, and we'll cover what you need to know as we move along. Just do it this way, and you can read about the boring stuff later on to find the answers for anything we didn't cover. Trust me, you don't need to know all those details now. You just want to make web pages, not win HTML trivia night at the local sports bar.

What Was All That About?

See, that wasn't so tough, was it? Don't worry, we will not be continuing on with the ridiculous battlefield metaphor, that was just for shock value to get you started. I just wanted a way to get your attention, so you could just dive right in, with a battle cry, cradling your keyboard like a rifle. You didn't need me telling you what all that stuff in the brackets meant, or why you had to type everything in that order. The bottom line is, it worked, regardless of your inexperience in the subject, so don't get bogged down with the details yet. You are not training to become a senior level web developer (crawl before you can walk), so let's not worry about all the academic stuff just yet.

The code you typed out above is HTML, which stands for Hyper Text Markup Language. It is the language that all web browsers use to interpret and display all web sites and pages. You will be learning the 5th version, or HTML5, which is the most current version in use today. It consists of a number of *tags* enclosed in brackets which let the browser know what each element is, and how to display it. The actual content to be used or displayed by the browser, is surrounded by a pair of tags, with the end tag containing a slash before the tag name (<title></title>). The tags themselves aren't displayed, and only serve as instructions to the browser, to let it know what each section is intended to do or show. This is something you should keep in mind as you are creating your pages, so you can understand how the browser will read the code as you build the page. Before moving on, let's take a moment to go over the tags used in the above example.

The Tags You Just Used

`<!DOCTYPE html>`

This is the first thing you have always got to type into any web page you create. It is not an HTML tag, but an instructional command sent to the browser, to let it know which version of HTML you are using. Previous versions of the DOCTYPE tag were long, complex and boring. Since HTML5 is the most current version, and only requires the version set as "html", don't even waste time worrying about previous methods.

`<html></html>`

Everything that the web browser will need to know or display in your page will be inside this element. Every aspect of the page, as far as what it does, and what it will look like, is contained between the opening and closing *html* tag.

`<head></head>`

Think of the *head* tag like the "thoughts" of the page (inside your head, see?). Anything you put in here, with the exception of the title tag, will not be displayed to the user. Content inside the head tags is used to modify, control and communicate behind the scenes information about the web page.

`<title></title>`

The title of your page. The tag is pretty self-explanatory. This is what appears in the title bar, or tab of the browser you use to view the page. It is the only content in the head tag that will be visible to the visitor.

`<body></body>`

All of the content that will be displayed to anyone viewing the page will be inside this tag. If the head tag is like the thoughts, then think of the body tag as the actions. The stuff that people will see. The content inside the body tag will generally make up most of your HTML document. At least for now.

All of the text outside of the brackets (but between the tag's opening and closing) is the actual content that the browser will display, or somehow communicate to the visitor. You will also notice that the content inside each tag is *nested* inside other of tag. This is important, since you want to make sure the browser reads everything in order, so it knows how to display the content, without messing anything up. Keep your code clean...you will thank me later.

This book was created to teach you some fundamental and usable skills in HTML and CSS (Cascading Style Sheets, which will be covered later), relatively quickly. This approach, of just diving right in to writing code, and seeing what works, is the same approach that I used when learning how to make web sites. Many other web designers and developers over the years have picked up their skills, or advanced their knowledge in the same way. However, this book will serve as your guide, so your journey will be more controlled, and your "diving" will be aimed in the right direction for building skills quickly, and not wasting time worrying about *why* just yet. We are here to actually use HTML, not just read about it.

When you are working with the code samples in this book, you should be typing out everything yourself. It is a great way to improve your typing skills, as well as forcing you to think about which tags you are using and where you are putting them. This will help you commit them to memory much quicker.

Keep in mind that this approach will not be teaching everything you need to know to make the best, most creative web sites, perfectly optimized for search engines. It is designed to give you all the skills you need to figure out things as you go, and at the same time, avoid many of the mistakes and bad habits that others have developed over the years. You don't need to spend months in a classroom, or weeks reading a super thick textbook. This is a specific, and targeted approach, that will let you develop only the skills you need to start building nice clean web pages without all the intimidation of the history behind it. You could easily complete the lessons in this book in one or two days if you dedicate the time.

Fundamentals of Battlefield HTML

We are going to start your next page, but rather than using what you just did, let's start over again. I heard that collective groan, but seriously, its not like you did much yet anyway. This will be a good way to practice typing everything out, as well as building a good directory structure that will make sense when you are working on much larger and more complex web sites.

Create a new folder and give it a name reminding you that your HTML files will be located there. Something like "myNewWebSite". Now open up your plain text editor of choice (Notepad or TextEdit), and create a new file. Name the new file index.html, and save it into the folder you just created. Now type all of the following code into the file:

```
<!DOCTYPE html>
<html>
  <!-- This is the head content -->
  <head>
    <title>BATTLEFIELD HTML: Markup in Mean
    Streets</title>
  </head>

  <!-- This is the body content -->
  <body>
    <!-- Main header and sub header for the page -->
    <h1>BATTLEFIELD HTML and CSS</h1>
    <h2>Markup in the Mean Streets</h2>

    <!-- Body copy for the page -->
    <p>This is the body copy for the web page you will
    be working with. Having more content in here
```

```
really shows how valuable some of the formatting
options are, so you should probably ramble in this
section a bit. You can also just copy and paste a
chunk of text that you  type out, in order to pad
this section. Hey are you still reading this?</p>

<!-- This sentence contains a link tag (a) -->
<p>Are you ready? Well then, <a href="#">let's
roll!</a></p>
</body>
</html>
```

Once again, you can open your favorite web browser, and take a look at how the page is displayed. While tags in HTML5 are not case sensitive, it is a good idea to keep the tags all lower case, so in the event that the code is used in a different environment that has case sensitivity (like XHTML), you will avoid many issues. There are several new tags being used in this page. We have added comments, header tags (not head), and anchor (hyperlink) tags. Let's just go over them briefly, to give you an idea of what they are doing there.

THE NEW TAGS

```
<!-- comment tags -->
```

Comment tags are used by the author of the page, in order to clearly note what each section of the code represents. It is extremely helpful to put comments into a page that you will be passing off for others to work with, since they can use the comments to get a feel for what you have intended. Comments in the above example aren't really needed, since the tags are easy to figure out, and the page isn't all that complicated. We are just covering them, so you have a tool that you can use in your own practice. Also, you will notice that comment tags don't need to be closed, like other tags.

`<h1></h1>` and `<h2></h2>`

Header tags are used just like header styles would be used in a Word document. In HTML, there are actually 6 levels of headers at your disposal (h1 – h6). The largest is h1, and the smallest is h6.

`<p></p>`

This is the paragraph tag, and is used like a carriage return in a word document. They start a new block of information on a new line.

`<a></a>`

Although they are represented with the letter "A", most people consider these hyperlink tags, but they are also known as anchor tags. This tag is used to add some interactivity to the page, allowing a visitor to navigate the site. Any content between the opening and closing tag becomes an interactive element, allowing the visitor to click on it. Right now it just contains a hash tag (#), which doesn't lead anywhere, but later we will be adding hyperlinks to navigate..

BLOCK ELEMENTS AND INLINE ELEMENTS

Now would be a good time to discuss block and inline elements, since we've reached a point where you will be using them in later lessons. For clarification, we will consider an element all of the content inside the opening and closing of a tag, as well as the tag itself.

Block elements are displayed on a new line. In the above code, the block elements are tags like header and paragraph tags. For example, two <p></p> elements placed one after another will be displayed on separate lines (the first on top of the second), rather than side by side.

Inline elements are tags that don't affect the flow of the content, and are displayed on the same line. Notice, the anchor tags in the code sample are nested inside a paragraph tag. When the page is viewed, the content is displayed on the same line as the rest of the content. Generally inline elements are used to enhance, distinguish, or otherwise differentiate the content it contains from the content it is displayed with. Tags that are considered inline elements include <b>, <i>, <span>, <strong>, and others that you will be able to play with later on. For now, just think of them as a way to modify the look of content, rather than where it is displayed.

The <img> Tag

Alright, now before we go any further, you are going to need two more files. Download the image files at the following site: http://brian-manning.com/battlefieldHTML/ (right click, *Save Image As...*). You will need to make a new folder in the same folder as your index.html page, and call it "images". Save the images in that folder, and add the following to your index.html code (in bold):

```
<!DOCTYPE html>
<html>
  <!-- This is the head content -->
  <head>
    <title>BATTLEFIELD HTML: Markup in Mean
    Streets</title>
  </head>

  <!-- This is the body content -->
  <body>
    <!-- Main header and sub header for the page -->
    <img src="images/title.png" width=500 height=40
    alt="title">
    <h2>Markup in the Mean Streets</h2>

    <img src="images/cats.jpg" width=300 height=400
    alt="cats">

    <!-- Body copy for the page -->
    <p>This is the body copy for...
  </body>
</html>
```

Notice above that you are replacing the <h1> content with a new tag, as well as adding another tag before the body copy. This is the image tag, and lets the browser know that you would like an image to be displayed there. The attribute *src* is the source of the file. In this case, you saved the files into a folder (directory) called *images*. You are now telling the browser to look in the images directory, and find the files by name. The height and width attributes are not required, but it is always a good idea to make note of the image file's dimensions, and put them into the tag. Just trust me for now, and you can worry about why this is important when you have a firm grasp on using the *img* tag. The *alt* tag is the alternate content that is displayed if the image doesn't load in the browser. It is also visible to search engines, so it is a good idea to include that for best results. Or not...I'm not your boss, so do what you want.

Like the comment tag, the img tag is also a single element that doesn't need to be closed. All of the information to display the image properly is contained within the brackets of the tag.

Develop Good Habits

When formatting HTML, it is essential to *nest* all of your tags properly. This means that you must open and close all of your tags inside the element that contains that tag. Let's take a look at an example of a properly nested set of tags:

```
<body>
   <p>This tag is <b>properly nested</b> inside of
   the  paragraph tag</p>
</body>
```

In the above sample, the *p* tag is properly nested, but also notice that the *span* tag is also nested, meaning that it is opened, then closed before the *p* tag that contains it, is closed. Don't do something like this:

```
<body>
   <p>This tag is not properly nested inside of the
   <b>paragraph tag</p></b>
</body>
```

Improper nesting will often break HTML pages, but sometimes it will work just fine without causing problems. Especially with inline elements. However, it is always considered incorrect, so nest those suckers right the first time, and we will not have to send the validation goon squad out for you.

Another helpful hint is to really make use of the comment tag. You will be nesting a lot of elements once you get deeper into web design, so make your life easier and comment your page well. One trick that will save time on the mouse wheel, is to comment the closing part of a tag, so you know what it is when you are further down the page. You will thank your past self when you don't need to scroll up to check where the tag was opened.

Fundamentals of BATTLEFIELD CSS

This is where things start heating up. You will learn about the *style* tag and Cascading Style Sheets (CSS) to apply rules, letting the browser know how and where certain elements should appear on the page. We will be keeping the same "shoot first, ask questions later" approach when learning all of this stuff, but I also encourage you to do plenty of research once you have got a solid grasp of what we will be covering.

Enough talk! Back to work! Now that we've got a healthy chunk of content sitting on the page, we can shift our focus away from the body element, and move up to the head element to add some flare to our page. For that, we are going to dive right into Cascading Style Sheets.

The Style Tag

The Style tag lets the browser know that everything within the tag defines how we want certain HTML elements on the page to be displayed. We will be using *Cascading Style Sheet (CSS)* definitions contained within the style tag. So in your html file, add the style tag inside the head element, after the title element.

```
<!DOCTYPE html>
<html>
<!-- This is the head content -->
<head>
   <title>BATTLEFIELD HTML: Markup in Mean
   Streets</title>
```

```
<style>
<!-- css styles used to change how the page looks
-->

</style>
</head>

<!-- This is the body content -->
<body>
    . . .
</body>
</html>
```

Time to take advantage of the power of CSS, and start dropping some code in there for more control. Everything that you will be adding now will go inside the style element that you just added. Also, make sure you include all of the punctuation exactly, since CSS code is stricter than HTML, so leaving out a semi-colon, or comma will break the style you are trying to apply to the elements in the page. Again, We'll just throw out a chunk of code that you will be typing, and then go over what you just did later. Let's get started, shall we? Inside the style element, type the following exactly as you see it:

```
<style>
<!-- css styles change how the page looks -->

body {
    color: #cccccc;
    background: #333333;
    margin: 24pt;
    font-family: verdana, sans-serif;
    font-size: 10pt;
```

```
}

h1 {
   color: #ff6600;
   font-size: 16pt;
   margin-bottom: -16pt;
}
h2 {
   color: #999999;
   font-size: 14pt;
}

p {
   width: 400px;
   border: dotted 1px #996600;
}

a {
   color: #cc6600;
}

</style>
```

Take a look at your page in the web browser. Looks much different now, right? Without even making any changes to the actual content inside the body tags, we were able to tell the browser how to display the various elements on the page. As you can see, several of the various tags we used are listed above, with bits of code contained within curly brackets.

Each line grouped inside the curly brackets is a CSS property, which gives you great control of how to display, position, and even interact with elements on the page. Make note of how the colon and semi-colon are used, since that is very important. The order is *property* then a colon, *value* then a semi-colon to let the style sheet know the declaration is complete.

The power of CSS and the style tag is that it gives you complete control over how a page and all its content is displayed, without actually having to edit the content itself. With this ability (and some planning and forethought), you can modify the entire layout of a site, using only CSS. Let's take a moment to discuss some of the properties we just used.

CSS Properties

`color`

This is the property used to determine the foreground or text color of the element.

`background`

Although we only used this property to set the background color of the entire page, there is a separate *background-color* property we could have used instead. But the background property itself allows to you define several aspects, like background images, opacity (alpha), and other aspects of the background.

`font-family and font-size`

As you would expect, these are used to determine which fonts to use, how large they should be displayed. In the font-family property, there are two attributes listed (separated by a comma...important). The first tells the browser to use the font "Verdana" if it is on the visitor's computer. Otherwise it will default to the browser's sans-serif font.

`margin and margin-bottom`

The margin property defines the space around the element, increasing (or decreasing in the case of negative values) the distance around that particular element. In case you were wondering, yes there is a margin-top, margin-left and margin-right property. The margin property itself can be used to set all four individually, though. We will cover that later.

`border`

This property puts a visible border around any element you apply it to. Several attributes are defined (*not* comma separated), but like margin, this property also has several sub properties you can use, like border-width.

Colors are defined using hexadecimal values (three 2-digit pairs with each digit in the pair containing 0-9 or a-f, preceded by a hash tag). There has always been a set of 216 "web safe" colors, which you can see at a site like http://www.html-color-codes.com. When in doubt, its not a bad idea to stick with that specific range (like the examples above have done). However, don't be afraid to try any of the 16 million color values possible within the hexadecimal range. Sites like http://www.color-hex.com or http://www.colorpicker.com are great web resources that help you find and pick colors by hexadecimal value.

CSS Power and Flexibility

Cascading style sheets give the author great control over how the page will be displayed. However, it is not perfect control, since the various browsers will interpret the properties differently, but it is more than enough to really nail down your vision. You will now get to take advantage of the flexibility. Copy all of the code that you typed in between the style tags (but not the style tags themselves), and open a new text document. Paste the content into the empty file. Create a new folder in the same folder as your index.html and images folder, and call it "css". Save the new document in there and give it the filename "style.css". You will be replacing the entire style element with the following code (in bold):

```
<!DOCTYPE html>
<html>
<!-- This is the head content -->
<head>
   <title>BATTLEFIELD HTML: Markup in Mean
   Streets</title>

   <link rel="stylesheet" type="css/text"
   href="css/style.css">
</head>

<!-- This is the body content -->
<body>
      . . .
</body>
</html>
```

Much like the image tag, the *link* tag tells the browser where to find your stylesheet file (style.css), and apply the styles to the page. You are linking to an external style sheet, so now you no longer need to have all of the style code in the head tag, making it much easier for you to apply the styles to page you make. Just add that line above into the head tag of every new page you make. The biggest strength of this external linking is that any changes you make to the stylesheet itself will be applied across every page that links to the file. Just so that there is no further confusion, your index.html page should now look like this:

```
<!DOCTYPE html>
<html>
<!-- This is the head content -->
<head>
    <title>BATTLEFIELD HTML: Markup in Mean Streets</title>

    <link rel="stylesheet" type="css/text" href="css/style.css">
</head>

<!-- This is the body content -->
<body>
    <!-- Main header and sub header for the page -->
    <img src="images/title.png" width=500 height=40 alt="title">
    <h2>Markup in the Mean Streets</h2>

    <img src="images/cats.jpg" width=300 height=400 alt="cats">

    <!-- Body copy for the page -->
    <p>This is the body copy for the web page you will be working with. Having more content in here
```

```
    really shows how valuable some of the formatting
    options are, so you should probably ramble in this
    section a bit. You can also just copy and paste a
    chunk of text that you   type out, in order to pad
    this section. Hey are you still reading this?</p>

    <!-- This sentence contains a link tag (a) -->
    <p>Are you ready? Well then, <a href="#">let's
    roll!</a></p>
</body>
</html>
```

Just take a moment to compare your code with the above, and since you will be jumping back and forth between the two files anyway, make sure your style.css file looks like this:

```
body {
   color: #cccccc;
   background: #333333;
   margin: 24pt;
   font-family: verdana, sans-serif;
   font-size: 10pt;
}

h1 {
   color: #ff6600;
   font-size: 16pt;
   margin-bottom: -16pt;
}
h2 {
   color: #999999;
   font-size: 14pt;
}

p {
   width: 400px;
```

```
  border: dotted 1px #996600;
}

a {
  color: #cc6600;
}
```

THE MIGHTY <DIV> TAG

There is one more tag we'll be using heavily. Probably more than the paragraph or image tags. The mighty *div* tag denotes a division of content. It is a block level element, so all of the content in the div element will appear, as a group, on a new line. This is going to be our go to tag when grouping and laying out content on the page, giving us the a greater level of control. So let's add a few to the index page (in bold):

```
<!-- This is the body content -->
<body>
   <!-- Main header and sub header for the page
   <div>
   <img src="images/title.png" … alt="title">
   <h2>Markup in the Mean Streets</h2>
   </div>

   <div>
      <img src="images/cats.jpg" … alt="cats">

      <!-- Body copy for the page
      <p>This is the body copy for the web page you
      will be working with. Having more content in
      here really shows how valuable some of the
      formatting options are, so you should probably
      ramble in this section a bit. You can also just
```

```
            copy and paste a chunk of text that you type
            out, in order to pad this section. Hey are you
            still reading this?</p>

            <!-- This sentence contains a link tag (a) -->
            <p>Are you ready? … <a href="#">let's roll!
            </a></p>
        </div>
    </body>
```

To apply a style to the div elements, add the following to your stylesheet (style.css). You can add it anywhere on the file, as long as it isn't inside another property's brackets:

```
div {
   width: 600px;
   border: solid 1px #ffffff;
   margin: auto;
}
```

Looking at your index page in a browser now shows the two groups (header content and regular content) wrapped in two separate boxes (div tags), with a single pixel white border (border property), floating in the center of the page (width and margin properties).

Fig. 1 This is what you should see in your browser. Or at least something close.

Let's Bring a Little Class to the Show

As you can see, the groups of tags have been repositioned by the <div> tags wrapping around them, but they themselves have remained relatively unchanged. We've achieved a great deal of control over the content on the page, but we can still do so much more. All of the styles we have defined are applied globally across all tags that we've included into the stylesheet. We need a way to control specific elements without affecting other elements with the same tags. Make the following tweak to your index page:

```
<div class="header">
   <img src="images/title.png" … alt="title">
   <h2>Markup in the Mean Streets</h2>
</div>
```

In order to take advantage of the new *class* label you added, make the following additions and modifications to your stylesheet (in bold):

```
p {
   width: 400px;
   border: dotted 1px #996600;
   margin: 5px auto;
}
…

div {
   width: 600px;
   border: solid 1px #ffffff;
   margin: auto;
   text-align: center;
}
div.header {
   background: #000000;
   margin-bottom: 10px;
}
```

What did you notice about the changes? The top div content now has a black background and some breathing room on the bottom (margin-bottom property). Also, adding the "align-text" property to the main div style has centered everything between the div tags. However, we had to add that "margin: 5px auto;" to the paragraph tag style, in order to get those to center properly (this trick is explained in later lessons).

Notice also, that the top div block still has its border and width, and all of the text inside the paragraph tags is now centered. This is because the styles *cascade* down from the parent style to anything inside the tag that the style is applied to. This gives you the ability to set attributes globally to a tag group, but at the same time you still have the ability to define a tag's *class* and apply styles to specific elements. But with great power, comes great responsibility. If you are going to apply styles in a broad stroke, you must be aware of how it will affect all other content as the styles cascade down to the child tags wrapped inside.

Congratulations! You now know enough HTML to build clean, nice-looking pages from scratch! Just enough to be dangerous, but you could go very far with what little you have picked up. We are going to add a few new techniques and elements to the tags you have used so far. From this point on, we will not be using this file anymore. It is always a good idea to practice typing out all of the tags, so you should build some new files to play around with. Until then, sit back and bask in the glory of your work (and one of the few pictures of my cats getting along).

Battlefield Applications

What we are going to do now is build two separate pages, using stylesheets to match a layout template as close as we can. These next two exercises are based off of somewhat common site layouts seen around the web today. The idea is to show you how easy it is to create and layout your web sites once you start getting a handle on HTML5 and CSS3. Just to keep it simple, we will not be using any images in these site templates, but that doesn't mean you have to exclude them. For the best results, build the pages, based on the example first. Once you feel comfortable with why everything is used the way it is, feel free to start messing around.

Before we go on, I want to point out something helpful when doing layouts that aren't build around actual content. We will be filling out sections using "dummy text". The most common filler for this is from classic Latin literature and is known in the design world as "Lorem Ipsum". It is very easy to find this filler text, but I personally use the site http://lipsum.com, because of the handy generator they've got on there.

The site is also a great resource to read up on the history of Lorem Ipsum, and why it is used (spoiler: it is so the client can focus on the layout and design, rather than the filler content). That is far beyond the scope of this book, so I do encourage you to check the site out if you are interested. For now, just head over there and grab some filler text.

Site Template 1

Again, I do highly recommend you start from the beginning, using a blank file. There are several reasons for this. First, you will be able to learn the tags and stylesheet properties much quicker if you type them out. Second, you will have a fresh page to work with, so there will be no confusion trying to manipulate all of the previous content. Finally, you will be able to keep your "first web site" safely unharmed, to look back upon after you have built your web design empire.

I put some layout compositions together using photoshop, so you can see (and plan for) what we have intended to do. It is always a good idea to work with a rough layout like this, so you are not blindly coding with no real plan. The easiest way is to sketch it out on a piece of paper. That makes it cheaper, faster, and you've already conquered the learning curve of pen and paper. Many web sites today started their lives on a napkin, sketched out with waitress' pen.

Fig. 2.1 This is the site layout we will be building in this exercise.

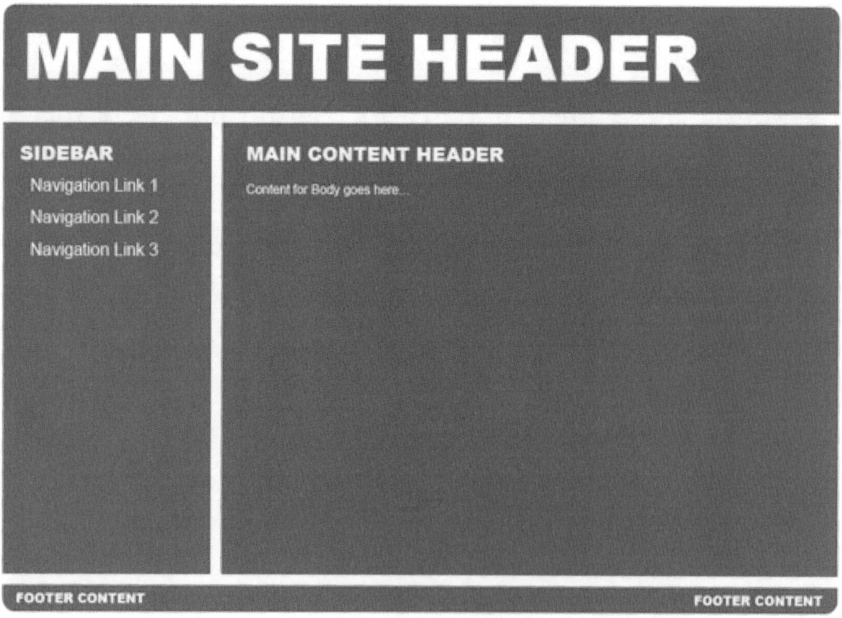

You know the routine, people. Open your favorite text editor, and create a new file. Type out all of the core tags you will need.

```
<!DOCTYPE html>
<html>
<head>
    <title>BattleField HTML - Exercise 1</title>
    <link rel="stylesheet" type="css/text" href="css/ex1.css">
</head>

<body>

</body>
</html>
```

Create a new directory called "exercise_1" and, as usual, save the file in there as index.html. Why are we still calling it index.html? Don't worry about it. You are not at the boring classroom part yet. Next you will have to create a stylesheet. Make a new directory called "css" and save a new blank file as "ex1.css" or whatever you want to call it. But you do have to make sure that you are placing it in the "css" directory. If you named the stylesheet something other than "ex1.css", you will have to update the *href* attribute of the link tag. Otherwise it will not know where to find the stylesheet, and you will be wasting time trying to figure out why.

We are going to start with the HTML first. Once that is complete, the next step will be to use a stylesheet to organize and display all of the content to match the template comp as close as we can.

```html
<body>
  <div id="header-bar">
    <h1>Site Layout Template 1</h1>
  </div>

  <div id="body-wrapper">

    <div id="sidebar">
      <h3>Site Navigation</h3>
      <div class="links">
      <a href="http://battlefieldHTML.com" class="nav-link">Home</a>
      <a href="http://google.com" class="nav-link">Search</a>
      <a href="http://amazon.com" class="nav-link">Shopping</a>
      <a href="http://brian-manning.com" class="nav-link">Other</a>
      </div>
    </div>

    <div id="body-content">
      <h2>Let's Build a Site Template!</h2>
      <p>Lorem ipsum dolor sit amet, consectetur …
         ...Nam eget augue ac massa viverra sagittis at in leo...
         ...Aliquam interdum aliquam accumsan.</p>
    </div>

    <div class="clear-float"></div>
  </div>

  <div id="footer">
```

```
        <h4>Footer content for the site</h4>
    </div>
</body>
```

Remember to save the file often, because they are free, and you never run out of saves. The Lorem Ipsum content inside the paragraph tag is where you will put your own dummy text. What we've done differently, is to use the attribute *id* instead of *class* which we were using before. You will be running into this stuff when you get deeper into web design and development, so its good to get used to using it now. Basically, the *id* property means that the element will only appear once on the page (one *header* one *footer*, etc).

Take a look at the "href" attributes in the hyperlink tags. We are now linking to other websites, outside of the page itself. These links are known as *absolute links* and always begin with *http://* to let the browser know that it is a different website. The other type of link, which is what you will most likely be using for your site's navigation, is a *relative link*. A relative link points to a page or file that is in the same relative directory structure as the page itself. The best example is your link tag in the head element. It is pointing to the directory "css" and the file "ex1.css" inside that directory. Since the directory "css" is in the same directory as the index page, you don't need anything preceding the location.

Now we should take a look at the stylesheet and see if we can make this page flow a little better. Go back to ex1.css (or whatever you named it), and type out the following:

```
body {
   font-family: arial, verdana, sans-serif;
   font-size: 12pt;
   color: #fff;
}

h1, h2, h3, h4 {
   margin: 0;
   padding: 0;
}
```

The styles above are setting properties globally across the entire page. These are the base style properties that the rest of the styles will inherit. These styles *cascade* down unless they are overridden by another style. We have gone over these properties before, but to refresh your memory, the property *font-family is* setting the font that the browser will use for the entire page, with three different options. If Arial is not available to the browser, it will use Verdana. However if that is unavailable, the browser will switch to its default sans-serif font. The *font-size* is set to 12 point type, which will be the base size all other styles will modify if necessary. The *color* is set to white (see **CSS Properties** for a brief explanation on hexadecimal color values). Since all three value pairs in the color property are matching, you can reduce them each to single digits (#fff instead of #ffffff).

In the next style declaration, you are setting the styles on multiple tags, separated by commas. In this case, you will be setting the margin and padding for all h1-h4 tags to zero. If you set the value of a property to zero, it is a good habit to leave off any measurement types, like pt (point), px (pixel), or percentages. Remember to separate the header tags with a comma in your style declaration.

The property, *padding* is new here. Much like margin, padding refers to the space around the element. Margin applies to the space outside of the element's boundaries (the gap between two elements), and padding applies to the space inside the boundaries (the gap between the edge of the element, and where the content sits). OK, now add the next two styles.

```
#header-bar {
   width: 770px;
   height: 50px;
   padding: 15px;
   margin: 10px auto;
   border-top-left-radius: 12px;
   border-top-right-radius: 12px;
   background: #559;
}
#header-bar h1 {
   font-size: 250%;
   margin-left: 15px;
   text-transform: uppercase;
}
```

When we were defining the style for a *class*, we used *dot notation*. For instance, when applying a class to a div tag, you would declare it as *div.classname*. For an id, a hash tag is used, and it is generally defined as its own style. You could declare a class style on its own as well (*.classname* instead of *div.classname*), but since classes can be used multiple times by multiple tags, it is best to use dot notation to specify a tag that the class will apply to.

The *#header-bar* style defines the size and other properties of the element containing the main title. I'm going to jump around a bit to explain a couple of things. First, we are setting the width to 770px, but the padding is set at 15px (pixels) all the way around. The padding adds an additional 30 pixels of width (15 pixels on the left and right), giving us a total width of 800 pixels. This also applies to the height. The padding for the top and bottom add an additional 30 pixels, and since the height is defined as *50px*, the total height for the header bar is 80 pixels.

When defining the margin property, there are two values. The first value, *10px*, represents the top and bottom values. The second value, *auto*, sets the left and right values, and in this case it is telling the browser to automatically fill in the left and right sides of the header-bar equally. When you have a defined width, and the left and right margins set to *auto*, the element will be centered on the page. Its a nice trick, so remember that. Also, if you want to set all four values to something different in the same declaration, you can use four values, which will apply in this order: *margin: [top] [right] [bottom] [left];* with each value separate by a space, not a comma.

In order to get the nice rounded corners, we are using a CSS3 property that is supported by every major browser now, making it much easier than before. Each corner is set individually using *border-top-left-radius* and *border-top-right-radius*. If you just used the property *border-radius*, it would affect all four corners, so we've got to call them out individually.

The value for the *background* property is only a three digit value (always preceded by the hash tag). This value is read as *#555599*. Remember, hexadecimal values consist of three pairs of values, with each pair representing red, green and blue (RGB). The value used for this property is defined as R(55), G(55), and B(99). Since each pair is a matching pair, you can reduce them to single digit values R(5) G(5) B(9), or *#559*. This can only be done if all three values are matching pairs. All 216 web-safe colors can be defined using this condensed method.

For the next style declaration, *#header-bar h1*, you are setting the style for all h1 tags inside the header-bar element. This will override any styles cascade to this element, if you define them here. For instance, we are changing the left margin on all h1 tags in the header-bar to add 15px of space. The font size is using a percentage, based off of the *font-size* property you set in the body style declaration. For this style, the h1 content will be 250% larger than the globally defined 12pt size. Finally, the last property should be easy to figure out; it is changing all of the text to all uppercase letters, regardless of what capitalization you put in there. Moving right along, let's define the style for the *body-wrapper* element.

```
#body-wrapper {
   width: 799px;
   padding: 0;
   margin: 0 auto;
   border: dotted #aaa;
```

```
    border-width: 0 0 0 1px;
}
```

The two properties we need to cover in this are *border* and *border-width*. The first, *border* is setting the style of border as a dotted line, and then setting its color (separated with a space, not a comma). The next, *border-width*, is defining the size of the border itself. We could have used *border-left-width*, which in most cases you should use if you are only changing a single side, but in this case we want to make sure that all other values are set to zero. Just like in the margin and padding properties, the values are defined in the order, top, right, bottom middle. Starting from the top, the values go in a clock-wise direction.

The width is a funky 799px, because, like the padding, the border's width affects the overall width. For this element, the padding on the left and right sides are zero, but the border on the left side is 1px. This gives us a total width of 800 pixels, like the header bar. Next we'll define the sidebar and body content.

```
#sidebar {
   width: 180px;
   margin: 0 9px 0 0;
   padding: 10px;
   float: left;
}

#sidebar a.nav-link {
   color: #999;
   text-decoration: none;
   margin: 10px;
   border: dotted #999;
   border-width: 0 0 1px 0;
```

```
    display: block;
}

body-content {
    width: 560px;
    padding: 10px 15px;
    float: left;
    background: #99c;
}
```

Since these two elements are all contained within the *#body-wrapper* element, we need to make sure that the total of all margins, padding, borders and widths for both the sidebar and body-content don't exceed 799px (the width that was set for *#body-wrapper*). Otherwise, they will not sit side-by-side. They can be under 799px, but then the edges will not match up to the edges of the header-bar, so we are shooting for exactly 799px.

One of the properties in both the sidebar and the body-content styles is *float: left*, which tells the browser that these should float on the left side, and all other content should wrap around the elements. If we didn't set the body-content to float to the left, then it could (and most likely will) push the element all the way to the left, and wrap its content (the h2 and p tag content) around the sidebar element. Setting them both to float will *stack* them from left to right. Since the two elements with content inside the *#body-wrapper* element float, there is nothing to determine an actual height for the body wrapper element. This causes some funky layout issues with elements further down the page trying to wrap around the floating content.

We've got to make a small fix. See the div tag with the class *clear-float*? We'll use that to help clear things up by adding this style.

```
div.clear-break {
   clear: both;
}
```

This will let the browser know that anything after this element will no longer wrap around floating elements. This trick, using multiple floats, allows designers to layout a page, so they can sometimes place the content in a more search-engine-friendly format. It can be used to put more important content closer to the top of the page (in the HTML code itself).

Just for clarification, the *#sidebar a.nav-link* style is there to alter the look of all hyperlink tags in the sidebar. We are removing the underline, typical with default hyperlinks, by using *text-decoration: none*, and adding a dotted underline instead. Also, by using *display: block*, we are forcing the next hyperlink to appear on a new line like a block element. It is using a specific class (*nav-link*) declared in the HTML, so that other hyperlinks that appear in the sidebar are unaffected. Finally to finish this up, just add the following (before the *div.clear-break* style to keep things clean).

```
footer {
   width: 780px;
   margin: 10px auto;
   padding: 0 10px;
   border-bottom-left-radius: 12px;
   border-bottom-right-radius: 12px;
```

```
    background: #559;
    font-size: 80%;
    text-align: right;
}
```

Now feel free to save it, and take a look at your page. If you didn't miss any of the semi-colons, and all of your values add up properly, you should have something that flows just like the template mockup from the beginning of the exercise.

Fig. 2.2 This is the answer you got on your test too, right?

Pat yourself on the back, and take a break. We'll move on to the next exercise soon enough, youngling.

Site Template 2

This template exercise will be reusing most of what we did in the previous exercise, but that doesn't mean you get to reuse the page from exercise 1. The elements will be nested differently, and new class labels will be use. You may as well just type it all out again, to prevent hair-pulling frustration. That's the type of headache you only want to deal with if there's a ton of content, and you can't effectively start over. No complaining, just do it, so you can get better.

Again, we start with the mockup to help you *visualize and attack* the HTML and CSS. This time the nav bar is moved up to the top, and the sidebar is floating on the right. This is a typical blog style layout with the large content section on the right containing blog posts, and the right side for things like ads, links to other blogs, and a more detailed site navigation. The stylesheet will handle most of these elements similar to how they were done in the first exercise, but there are a few different elements and styles that will expand on what we've done previously.

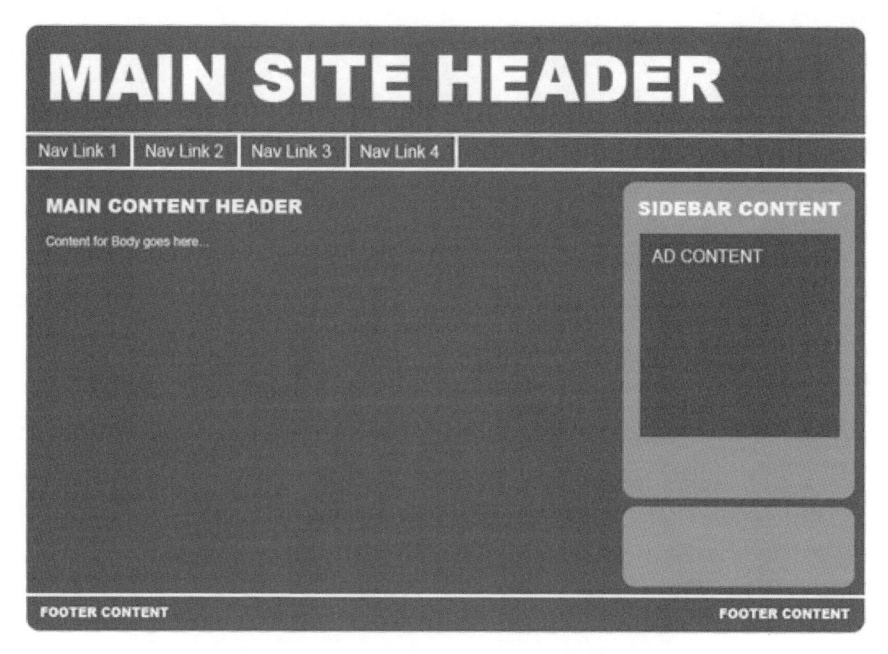

Fig. 3.1 This is the site layout we will be building in this exercise.

This is the last time I will have to mention this. Open your plain text editor, and start a new html file. If you were lazy, you would probably already have this part as a separate file to start with. But then you wouldn't have as much practice typing this stuff out, and you would find yourself looking it all up anyway. Just type it out. Trust me.

```
<!DOCTYPE html>
<html>
<head>
   <title>BattleField HTML - Exercise 2</title>
   <link rel="stylesheet" type="css/text"
   href="css/ex2.css">
</head>
```

```
<body>

</body>
</html>
```

Save that into a new directory called "exercise_2" and, as usual call it index.html. Now create a new stylesheet., saving it as "ex2.css" and remember to place it in a directory called "css" in the same directory as your index.html page. Of course you already knew all that, right? Just keeping you on your toes.

While some of the elements on this page will still be the same as before, we are going to do somethings a bit differently, so type out the following.

```
<body>
  <div id="header-bar">
    <h1>Site Layout Template 1</h1>
  </div>

  <div id="nav-bar">
  <div class="links">
  <div class="nav-link"><a href="#">Link 1</a></div>
  <div class="nav-link"><a href="#">Link 2</a></div>
  <div class="nav-link"><a href="#">Link 3</a></div>
  <div class="nav-link"><a href="#">Link 4</a></div>
  </div>

  <div class="tagline">www.BattleFieldHTML.com</div>
  <div class="clear-float"></div>
  </div>

  <div id="body-wrapper">
```

```html
    <div id="body-content">
      <h2>Let's Build a Site Template!</h2>
      <p>Lorem ipsum dolor sit amet, consectetur Nam
      eget augue ac massa viverra sagittis at in leo
      Aliquam interdum aliquam accumsan.</p>
    </div>

    <div id="sidebar">
      <div class="content">More Navigation Here</div>
      <div class="content"><div class="ad">Sidbar Ad
      Box</div></div>
    </div>

    <div class="clear-float"></div>
    </div>

    <div id="footer">
      <h4>Footer content for the site</h4>
    </div>
  </body>
```

Now for your stylesheet, you are going to be reusing several of the styles with slight changes. Go ahead and use the same style declarations for *html, body* and *h1, h2, h3, h4*. Yes, you can copy and past them, but wouldn't you feel better if you typed all that out again? You can also reuse *#header-bar* and *#header-bar h1*. You will need to make this slight change to the *#header-bar* style.

```
#header-bar {
    ...
    padding: 15px;
    margin: 10px auto 0 auto;
    ...
}
```

What you are doing is setting the margin on all four sides, with the right and left set for auto, for proper centering of the header bar. Now that we are using a top side navigation bar, you will need to create some styles to handle the links. In the stylesheet, add the following styles.

```css
#nav-bar {
   width: 800px;
   margin: 2px auto;
}
#nav-bar div.nav-link {
   width: 80px;
   height: 18px;
   margin: 0 2px 0 0;
   padding: 5px;
   background: #559;
   text-align: center;
   float: left;
}
#nav-bar div.nav-link a {
   color: #fc0;
   text-decoration: none;
}
#nav-bar div.nav-link a:hover {
   color: #f60;
}
#nav-bar div.tagline {
   width: 408px;
   height: 18px;
   padding: 5px 12px;
   text-align: right;
   background: #559;
   float: left;
}
```

I'll go over these step by step, but the main point is that these styles have defined the top bar navigation element on the page. The *#nav-bar* style contains the whole element, so it is set to 800px with an automatic left and right margin. The '*#nav-bar div.nav-link*' style is used to only affect the div elements with the class *nav-link* inside the *#nav-bar* element. They are given a specific width, and set to float to the left, so that they can sit inline side-by-side.

Diving a bit deeper, the '*#nav-bar div.nav-link a*' style is used for the hyperlinks inside those div tags. The next one, '*#nav-bar div.nav-link a:hover*' sets the style for those hyperlinks when a user hovers the mouse pointer over them. Right now all we are doing is changing the color, to keep it simple.

Finally, the '*#nav-bar div.tagline*' style sets up the floating bar that fills in the rest of the *#nav-bar* element. The reason it has a specific width of 408px, is because that was the exact amount left over from the margins, widths, and padding from all of the other elements. We only do that, so the background color is flush with the rest of the elements down the right side of the page.

This template uses one uniform color across the width of the main content area, so we need to make a couple of changes to the *#body-wrapper* style. Now it should look like this

```
#body-wrapper {
    width: 800px;
    padding: 0;
```

```
   margin: 0 auto;
   background: #99c;
}
```

The *border* and *border-width* properties were no longer needed, so we can use the full 800px width. Also, the background color is set in this style, instead of the individual elements inside it. The *#body-content* style will also be pretty much the same as before, with some slight tweaks (not necessary to the actual flow of the page).

```
#body-content {
   width: 540px;
   padding: 20px 15px 10px 15px;
   float: left;
   text-align: justify;
   line-height: 150%;
}
```

The text has now been set to justified, rather than left, and now the line height (the space between lines) is set to 150% normal (1.5 line spacing). Moving on to the sidebar, there are some additions that need to be made.

```
#sidebar {
   width: 230px;
   margin: 0;
   padding: 10px 0;
   float: left;
}
#sidebar div.content {
   width: 200px;
   min-height: 45px;
   margin: 10px auto 0 auto;
```

```
    padding: 10px 10px 3px 10px;
    border-radius: 6px;
    color: #559;
    background: #ccf;
}
#sidebar div.ad {
    width: 85%;
    height: 120px;
    margin: 12px auto;
    padding: 10px;
    color: #fff;
    background: #000;
    border: solid 1px #fc0;
}
```

The major difference between this sidebar and the one from exercise 1 is the content that now sits inside the element. The *'#sidebar div.content'* style creates a box with rounded corners for the content. You have seen all of the other properties, except for *min-height*, which sets the minimum height for the element. It will stretch to contain anything beyond that, though.

The style *'#sidebar div.ad'* is only there to show what an ad box would look like in there. Actual ad content will generally contain its own styles, and will only require size and placement styling.

The footer from exercise 1 will still be used for this template as well. But in order to get the tighter margins between elements, you will need to add one additional style.

```
#footer p {
   margin: 0;
   padding: 0;
}
```

This style declaration prevents the p tag's padding and margin from spilling outside of the footer element, creating too much space between the footer and body wrapper.

Congratulations! You have finished your Web Design Boot Camp. Now you are ready to head out and create the next great website. Fly, young birdy. Fly and explore the world wide web (do people still say that?). You should now have a pretty solid grasp of what web design is all about. This is the point at which you can start looking up more tags, properties, and history of what's going on, because you will be able to understand what most of it means. Like the black belt rank in Karate, you are now ready to start learning.

CSS Background Images

We covered using images (img tag) in the most common way, but using CSS, we will be going over how to use images in the background of elements on the page. This will allow you to use images to make the page look nice, without having them actually take up any room on the page itself.

This time, we will be working from existing files, so no need to type it all out from scratch. You will be able to dig into existing code and see how you can use background images all through *cascading style sheets*. Of course, if you want to type it all out, it will be good practice.

The Sample Files

As I mentioned earlier, you will be working from an existing set of fles. Just head to **http://battlefieldhtml.com/ex3** and download the zip file you will find there. When you unzip the file, you can place it anywhere you like, but just to make your life easier, why don't you just put it in the same directory as all of your other exercise files.

> *For those of you that still want to type out the code, I'll include all of that at the end of this chapter. You will still need to download the zip file from the link above for the image files.*

Now take a look at the index.html page. It is very simple, straight forward and nothing that you can't figure out, just by looking at it. However, there is a new tag in there.

```
<header></header>
```

This tag is different than a page's main header, which contains the site's masthead and site navigation. The *header* tag can be added to different sections on the page that may need a heading tag, or other title for that section. As the actual use should be for, "a group of introductory or navigational aids". If you use any of the heading tags (h1, h2, ETC), you can place them inside your header tag, along with any other heading tags. This is also where you would place other information like the author of a blog post, or date it was published, along with corresponding links.

Other than the *header* tag, we will spend the most time in the style sheet. Open up "ex3_style.css", and take a good look at a perfectly formatted style sheet. If you downloaded the one from the link I provided above, then you'll just have to imagine it is perfectly formatted.

Most of the content in the file is there for placement purposes, to control how the content sits on the page. You will only have to look at the *background* style. It is the same as we've used in previous examples, but instead of using a hexadecimal color value, we will be pointing to an image file.

The background styles are calling an image using *relative* links, just like we discussed in chapter 6. The image's location is relative to the style sheet's location, so when you see this: "../" that is telling the browser to go back up one directory. Taking a closer look at the body style, you see this line.

```
background: url(../images/pageBG.gif) repeat-x;
```

What this means is, from the location of the style sheet (inside the css directory), go up one level. That will put you in the same location as the index.html file. Now go into the *images* directory and use the image called "pageBG.gif".

The next part of that line is *repeat-x*. The pageBG.gif file is the glossy blue bar that runs along the top of the page. Since we only want that to tile along the top row, you will set the repeat to only go along the x axis (horizontally). The other options for repeating a background images include:

- *repeat-y*, which tiles the image along the y axis
- *repeat*, which will tile along both the x and y axis
- *no-repeat*, which will only place the image once.

The background style for *main-container* uses the image "bodyBG.jpg" which is the large notebook paper image that all of the content will sit on. It makes the page look much more polished when you can do something as simple as a nice clean background image. If you notice, it is set to no-repeat, so the image is only placed once. One note, you need to set the main container's dimensions to match the width and height of the image itself, if you want the whole thing to show up. In this instance, the min-height style is used.

finally, the *header* style declaration uses the image "headerBG.png" to set the background image for the header tag content. Again, this does not repeat, since we only want it to show up once.

Take some time to dig into the style sheet to get a feel for the other properties as well. Everything else in the style sheet is used to control the precise placement, so the content can take advantage of the background image. The image is a piece of lined notebook paper, so since we know the distance between each blue line (20 pixels), we can set the font size and line height to ensure the content sits on the line, for a nice subtle effect.

For mobile browsers, the image and font sizes can sometimes be handled differently, so this type of effect is very difficult to maintain across all browsers. But it is a neat little trick to use for standard web browsers, so you can pick up a few tricks for your HTML playbook.

EXTRA CREDIT

The following excerpts are for those of you that still want to practice typing out all of the code. Here is all the code for both the *index.html* and *ex3_style.css* files contained in the zip file for this exercise.

INDEX.HTML

```
<!DOCTYPE html>
<html>
<head>
    <title>Battlefield HTML: Exercise 3</title>
```

```html
        <link href="css/ex3_style.css" rel="stylesheet"
        type="text/css">
    </head>
    <body>
        <div id="main-container">
            <div id="content-container">
                <header>Setting background images</header>
                <p>The purpose of this exercise is to use
                background images in a different way than the
                typical repeating tiled background of
                websites from the past. The page itself has a
                background image that is set to only repeat
                horizontally. The content below sits inside
                another container wrapped in a <em>div</em>
                tag, and has a background image that does not
                repeat.</p>

                <header>repeating images</header>
                <p>The two background images sit on top of
                each other, and appear seamless. Even with
                the browser window is stretched horizontally.
                The container stays centered, and the top bar
                fills the rest of the space.</p>

                <p>Also, since we know the distance between
                the lines on the notebook paper background
                (20 pixels), once we figure out the proper
                placement of the first line of text, we are
                able to style the text to sit on the lines.
                This will work with most browsers, however
                mobile browsers won't always size the text
                properly for this effect to work.</p>
            </div> <!-- content-container -->
        </div> <!-- main-container -->
    </body>
</html>
```

EX3_STYLE.CSS

Remember to save this as *ex3_style.css* in a directory called "css", so the browser knows where to find it when displaying the page.

```css
html, body {
   background-color: #fff;
   margin: 0;
   padding: 0;
   font-family: verdana, arial, sans-serif;
   font-size: 12pt;
   color: #302530;
}
body {
   background: url(../images/pageBG.gif) repeat-x;
}
header {
   width: 100%;
   height: 20px;
   margin: 0 0 0 -15px;
   padding-left: 15px;
   background: url(../images/headerBG.png) no-repeat;
   color: #fff;
   font-family: 'arial black';
   text-transform: uppercase;
}
#main-container {
   width: 830px;
   min-height: 450px;
   margin: 0 auto;
   padding-top: 130px;
   background: url(../images/bodyBG.jpg) no-repeat;
}
#content-container {
   width: 600px;
```

```
  margin: 0 auto;
  padding: 0 10px;
  line-height: 20px;
}
#content-container p {
  margin: 0 0 17px 0;
  padding-top: 3px;
}
```

Tags for Grown-up HTML

Up to this point, we have been able to accomplish a lot using the tags you've encountered. You could easily spend your whole web design career leaning heavily on the *div* tag, and style sheets to maneuver, place and design your web pages. On the surface, no visitor will be able to tell what tags you used to put the page together. It is the style sheets that do all the work for you anyway.

However, there are a few tags you can add to your arsenal, that won't affect the way you layout your page, as far as tag nesting is concerned. Just a few places that you can swap out the div tags, so your pages follow a universal standard. These are tags that let browsers, apps and other automated, or aggregate systems know what each part of your web page is intended to represent. It is the type of standard that allows you to share your content with other sites easily, without any additional work on your part.

The standards for these new tags has been defined by the World Wide Web Consortium (W3C), an organization that aims to set standards for HTML usage, in order to ensure wide accessibility internationally. The W3C has put several standards into place for the newer tags in HTML5, so it is in our best interest to adhere to them if you plan on incorporating them into your design.

Article and Section Tags

`<article></article>`

The *article* element is mainly used for things like blog entries, news posts, and other content that is meant to stand alone as a complete piece. Or as the W3C spec says: *"The article element represents a component of a page that consists of a self-contained composition in a document, page, application, or site and that is intended to be independently distributable or reusable, e.g. in syndication. This could be a forum post, a magazine or newspaper article, a blog entry, a user-submitted comment, an interactive widget or gadget, or any other independent item of content."*

What this means for you, is that anything that you would associate with a complete blog post, or news story will be contained within the article tag. Including the title, author, date of publication, the story itself, and even comments.

`<section></section>`

The *section* element, like the article element is meant to represent an independent block of related content. Unlike the article element, it does not necessarily include things like a title, or footer. In fact, the section element can be used to contain a collection of articles, or even just a part of an article, like the comments section.

There seems to be some debate over the use of the section and article elements. I don't really stand on any side of the debate, so what is covered here shouldn't be treated as the final word on the subject. I only aim to show you some common usage of the section element, along with the article element.

OTHER USEFUL TAGS

Other than the article and section tags, there are a number of other tags that you may be using for grouping content. If you choose to use these tags is up to you. Just keep in mind, understanding these standardized tags will help you layout the page in a way that will make it easier to understand what each section of your code is for. Getting away from the *div* tag is probably ideal if you wish to share your content outside of your web pages. Here are few more grouping elements.

`<nav></nav>`

Earlier techniques we have used to create a navigation section involved the mighty div tag. The *nav* element will let you group your links with a more semantically correct tag. This tag should be used for any major navigation elements on the page, leading to other sites, pages, or sections on the current page. It isn't necessary to use it for a simple grouping of links that aren't important to navigating your site.

`<aside></aside>`

The *aside* element is used for information that is tangentially related to the main content of an article, or any content on the page, that can still be separated from that content. Things like pull quotes, sidebars, or navigation to similar information.

```
<footer></footer>
```

Like earlier projects when we used a div tag to create the footer, the *footer* element is used the same way. It generally contains copyright information, licensing information, and links to related content or home page. It can be used within article and section elements as well, since those elements will sometimes contain footer appropriate content.

If we were to take the code from an earlier example, template 2, and swap out some of the div tags, this is one way you could use some of the new tags.

```
<body>
<header>
   <h1>Site Layout Template 1</h1>
</header>

<nav>
   <section class="links">
   <div class="nav-link"><a href="#">Link 1</a></div>
   <div class="nav-link"><a href="#">Link 2</a></div>
   <div class="nav-link"><a href="#">Link 3</a></div>
   <div class="nav-link"><a href="#">Link 4</a></div>
   </section>

   <div class="tagline">www.BattleFieldHTML.com</div>
   <div class="clear-float"></div>
</nav>

<div id="body-wrapper">
   <section id="body-content">
      <h2>Let's Build a Site Template!</h2>
```

```
    <p>Lorem ipsum dolor sit amet, consectetur Nam
    eget augue ac massa viverra sagittis at in leo
    Aliquam interdum aliquam accumsan.</p>
  </section>

  <aside>
    <div class="content">More Navigation Here</div>
    <div class="content"><div class="ad">Sidbar Ad
    Box</div></div>
  </aside>

  <div class="clear-float"></div>
</div>

<footer>
  <h4>Footer content for the site</h4>
</footer>
</body>
```

This is a quick example showing how you can incorporate some of the newer elements into previous designs. It is much easier to plan the page out, and use the new tags accordingly. Notice, though, that you can still declare *class* and *id* style definitions inside the tags, just like any other tag on the page. Don't let these tags intimidate you. They are only there to give meaning to the different ways content is generally grouped on a web page.

Finally, let's just go over a sample chunk of code, using a few of the newer tags. This way, you have a good idea how you can group your content in a way that makes sense to you, just by reading through the code.

```
<article>
  <header>
    <h3>Title of Post</h3>
    <h5>written by "Author"</h5>
  </header>

  <div class="content">
    <p>Lorem ipsum dolor sit amet, consectetur ...
    ...Nam eget augue ac massa at in leo...</p>
  </div>

  <section>
    <h4>2 comments for "Title of Post"</h4>
    <div class="comment">
      <a href="(link to user profile)">The Dude</a>
      <p>blah blah comment</p>
    </div>
    <div class="comment">
      <a href="(link to user profile)">Dude 2</a>
      <p>blah blah comment</p>
    </div>
  </section>

  <footer>
    <a href="../">Back to index...</a>
  </footer>
</article>
```

Remember, learning HTML is your own personal journey. Which is why you have picked up this book to learn, rather than spending weeks in a classroom. It is completely up to you how far you want to take your code. If you would rather leave the newer tags to the pro bloggers and online journalists (or at least to the people that are designing the backend code to generate the pages), that is fine. Don't let anyone else tell you how you should be designing a web page, if you are happy with the results.

If you want to take that next step, you've got all the tools necessary to make sense of anything thrown your way. Once you get the hang of everything in this book, you can expand your skills easily.

So, Uh...What Now What?

This whole "doing, not learning" method is only meant as a fast way to dive right in and start building web pages. It was never meant to be a replacement for actual studying of HTML and CSS, no matter how much I made it sound that way. The aim of this book has always been to get you familiar with the core tags and style properties, so that when you moved on to more advanced reading on the subjects, you would be able to figure out what those books and articles were trying to say.

It is clear that people learn a lot faster by doing, rather than reading about doing. With something like web design, it is very safe to play around and learn, using local files. You can spend a lot of time building pages that will never see the light of day, so you can go nuts trying everything out, with no fear of ruining an actual live web site.

What's next? This is the section of the book with resources for you to finally start making some sense of why you were doing things the way they were spelled out in the book. You will even learn the better ways to accomplish this, and in doing so, develop your own style. I'll also include links for some of the sites I like to visit, or reference, as well as some tools that I've used over the years to make this easier. Or you can keep using a simple text editor, and brag about it daily on Twitter.

This part will not be too long. I think part of your journey is finding the sites and tools that YOU like to use. Again, learn by using, not because I told you so.

Site Resources

http://www.smashingmachine.com – This is a great site that has a lot of very helpful articles and links to tips, tricks and tools that will help you better understand web design, and keep up with current trends.

http://www.w3schools.com/ - Although this site is also all about learning HTML and CSS, its approach tends to be a bit wordy, and broken up. However, as a resource for referencing all of the HTML tags, and CSS properties, complete with current browser compatibility, it is still a great site.

Coding Tools

The following are various text editors that will make typing out your HTML and CSS pages much easier. They have features like code/tag completion, and syntax highlighting that make it less painful to look at the mass of tags on the page. The best part is that they are all free.

> **NotePad++** (Windows) – This is the text editor that I hear most often suggested. It is free, but it has a simple yet slick design and still has a lot of features and power to serve you well. Available at http://notepad-plus.sourceforge.net
>
> **Text Wrangler** (Mac) – As a Mac user, this is the editor that is generally tossed about. It was the first one I used (actually it was the "older brother" BBEdit), and even after years of

use, I never really touched all the features its got. Available at http://www.barebones.com/products/textwrangler/

Komodo Edit (Windows, Mac, Linux) – This is the text editor I use the most now. No real reason I switched. I just liked how it handled HTML, as well as the languages I may have found myself using, like PHP, JavaScript, CSS, etc. Available at http://www.activestate.com/komodo-edit

About the Author

Brian Manning lives in Las Vegas, collecting many amazing adventures in the suburbs (Yes there are suburbs in Vegas). Unfortunately, he can't write any of them down, because *What Happens in Vegas, Stays in Vegas.*

If you would like to be informed automatically, by email, when Brian's next book is released, or for general updates, sign up at **brian-manning.com/newsletter.html**. Your email will never be shared, and you can unsubscribe at any time.

Word-of-mouth is crucial for any independent author to succeed. If you enjoyed this book, please consider leaving a review at Amazon, even if it's only a like or two. It would make all the difference and would be very much appreciated. For links to his books, you can visit Brian's Amazon.com Author Central Page at **amazon.com/author/brianmanning**

Thank you for taking the time to read this. If you liked it, and would like to say hi, or let Brian know what you thought, you can find him on Facebook (facebook.com/brian.manning2) and Twitter (@EvilTwinBrian).

BRIAN MANNING got his start doing web design before finishing the class he took to learn HTML in 1996. He learned more about web design the first couple of weeks working for the small web design company than he did that entire semester. His final class project was an eyesore, that did almost everything wrong, but it is still fondly remembered for the lessons it taught of what not to do. Brian has spent the better part of the last 15 years making websites and working with blogging templates for sites like Tumblr, and Wordpress.

Brian also has skills in Graphic Design, using software like Adobe Photoshop and Adobe Illustrator, and has also spent a number of years studying various martial arts, like Northern Shaolin Kung Fu, and Brazilian Jiu Jitsu. While those two areas seem very different, it was in those areas that he also realized the value of "doing, and not reading about doing" as the best approach to learning a new skill set.

Thank You!

This book started as a way of teaching my own boys (12 and 9 at the time of this writing) how to do HTML. I sat them down and went over the basics, and my oldest son suggested I write a book, since I seemed to know so much about it. Since I'm not some hot shot, high level web designer I sort of laughed it off. After that evening, I put some thought into it, and even though I don't have any high level degrees, or accomplishments, I've got over a decade of experience, and I am 99% self-taught. This book is my entire experience learning how to make web pages, boiled down into this condensed plan of attack that you are reading today.

I just want to say thank you for taking the time to read through this, and I really hope you have learned something using this approach. When you find a better way to do some of what we covered here, and you WILL find a better way, I hope you still look back fondly on the pages you built using the skills you picked up here, and remember how easy it all was, once you just started doing it.

Printed in Great Britain
by Amazon.co.uk, Ltd.,
Marston Gate.